STAND UP  SPEA

INDIGENOUS RIGHTS

Virginia Loh-Hagan

PROTECT —our— LAND

WE MATTER

Respect OUR Culture

Native VOTES COUNT

45TH PARALLEL PRESS

Published in the United States of America by Cherry Lake Publishing Group
Ann Arbor, Michigan
www.cherrylakepublishing.com

Reading Adviser: Beth Walker Gambro, MS, Ed., Reading Consultant, Yorkville, IL
Content Adviser: June Thiele
Book Designer: Jen Wahi

Photo Credits: © Rena Schild/Shutterstock.com, 4, 11, 30; © Diego G Diaz/Shutterstock.com, 6; © Courtesy of Amplifier.
org, 8; © Pierre Jean Durieu/Shutterstock.com, 12; © Pat Casper Photo/Shutterstock.com, 14; © miker/Shutterstock.com,
17, 18; © Chess Ocampo/Shutterstock.com, 20; © R.M. Nunes/Shutterstock.com, 23; © Dee Browning/Shutterstock.com,
24; © Alexey Suloev/Shutterstock.com, 26; © Chris Finch Photography/Shutterstock.com, 29, additional cover images
courtesy of iStock.com

45th Parallel Press is an imprint of Cherry Lake Publishing Group.

Library of Congress Cataloging-in-Publication Data

Names: Loh-Hagan, Virginia, author.
Title: Indigenous rights / Virginia Loh-Hagan.
Description: Ann Arbor, Michigan : Cherry Lake Publishing, [2021] | Series:
   Stand up, speak out | Includes bibliographical references and index.
Identifiers: LCCN 2021004995 (print) | LCCN 2021004996 (ebook) | ISBN
   9781534187559 (hardcover) | ISBN 9781534188952 (paperback) | ISBN
   9781534190351 (pdf) | ISBN 9781534191754 (ebook)
Subjects: LCSH: Indigenous peoples–Legal status, laws, etc.–Juvenile
   literature. | Indigenous peoples–Politics and government–Juvenile
   literature.
Classification: LCC KI80 .L64 2021 (print) | LCC KI80 (ebook) | DDC
   323.11–dc23
LC record available at https://lccn.loc.gov/2021004995
LC ebook record available at https://lccn.loc.gov/2021004996

Printed in the United States of America
Corporate Graphics

About the Author:

Dr. Virginia Loh-Hagan is an author, university professor, and former classroom teacher. She's currently the Director of the Asian Pacific Islander Desi American Resource Center at San Diego State University. She lives on the land of the Kumeyaay people. She lives with her very tall husband and very naughty dogs.

TABLE OF CONTENTS

Activists often work as a group. They have power in numbers.

WHAT ARE INDIGENOUS RIGHTS?

Everyone has the power to make our world a better place. A person just has to act. **Activists** fight for change. They fight for their beliefs. They see unfair things. They want to correct wrongs. They want **justice**. Justice is upholding what is right. Activists help others. They serve people and communities.

There are many problems in the world. Activists seek to solve these problems. They learn all they can. They raise awareness. They take action. They inspire others to act.

Activists care very deeply about their **causes**. Causes are principles, aims, or movements. They give rise to activism.

Many activists feel strongly about **Indigenous** rights. Indigenous means native. Indigenous people are the first to live in an area. They have their own ways of living. They have their own knowledge. They have their own beliefs.

Indigenous people fought against **colonization**. Colonization is the forceful takeover by another country or group of settlers. The colonizers took their land. They pushed out the Indigenous people, who were forced to change their lives. Today, Indigenous people are still mistreated. They're not given the same rights.

In this book, we share examples of Indigenous rights issues and actions. We also share tips for how to engage. Your activist journey starts here!

● The world has more than 370 million Indigenous people living across 90 countries.

GET STARTED

Community service is about helping others. It's about creating a kinder world. Activism goes beyond service. It's about making a fairer and more just world. It involves acting and fighting for change. Choose to be an activist!

○ **Focus on your cause!** In addition to the topics covered in this book, there are many others. Other examples include protecting Indigenous women and improving health care.

○ **Do your research!** Learn all you can about the cause. Learn about the history. Learn from other activists.

○ **Make a plan!** Get organized.

○ **Make it happen!** Act! There are many ways to act. Activists write letters. They write petitions. They protest. They march in the streets. They perform art to make people aware. They post to social media. They fight to change laws. They organize sit-in events. They participate in demonstrations and strikes. During strikes, people protest by refusing to do something, such as work.

WE THE RESILIENT

HAVE BEEN HERE BEFORE

Indigenous people should be celebrated more than 1 day a year.

CHAPTER 1

CELEBRATE INDIGENOUS PEOPLE

The second Monday in October is Columbus Day. Christopher Columbus was an Italian explorer. In 1492, he sailed to the Americas. Before Columbus, millions of people were already living in the Americas. Activists see Columbus as a colonizer. They want to celebrate Indigenous Peoples' Day instead. Indigenous Peoples' Day honors First Americans.

Several states have officially changed the name of the holiday. Anthony Tamez-Pochel is an activist. He's Cree and Lakota. He's from Chicago, Illinois. He formed the Chi-Nations Youth Council. He's fighting to replace Columbus Day in Chicago. He wants to change city law.

GET INSPIRED

BY INDIGENOUS RIGHTS ACTIVISM!

○ **Susan La Flesche Picotte** was the first Native American to earn a medical degree. She studied at the Women's Medical College of Pennsylvania. She graduated at the top of her class in 1889. She returned to her Omaha community. She built the first private hospital on a Native American reservation. A reservation is an area of land set aside by the U.S. government.

○ **Wilma Mankiller** became the first woman chief of the Cherokees in 1983. "Mankiller" is a term of respect. It refers to a fighter who guards villages. Mankiller helped her people. She improved health care. She improved education. She improved tribal government. She supported women's rights.

○ **Neville Bonner** was the first Indigenous person of Australia to serve in the Australian government. He was a businessman. He entered politics in 1971. He fought for Indigenous rights. He fought against drilling in the Great Barrier Reef and around the world.

Activists at the Indigenous Peoples March took a stand against issues that harm their lands, peoples, and cultures.

He said, "We don't need to celebrate someone who's committed **genocide**." Genocide is the killing of many people from a specific group. Genocide can also be the erasing of a culture. This is called cultural genocide.

Activists want to raise awareness about Native Americans. Jerry Elliot High Eagle is Cherokee and Osage. He worked on the U.S. space programs. In 1976, he created a law for Native American Awareness Week. In 1990, President George H. W. Bush declared November as National American Heritage Month.

There are many Native American heritage sites. Visit one to learn more.

The first Indigenous Peoples March took place on January 18, 2019. It happened in Washington, D.C. It was organized by the Indigenous Peoples Movement. Tribes, nations, and communities came. They united together to fight for justice. The event had speeches, prayers, songs, and dances. Marchers carried signs. A sign read, "We will not be silenced."

Stand Up, Speak Out

Not many people know about the injustices Indigenous people face. Indigenous cultures are at risk. Activists want to increase awareness. You can help!

> Host speaking events. Invite Indigenous people to talk about their cultures. Invite activists to talk about their causes. Host discussions. Talk with others about what you learned.

> Think about the history you've learned. You've probably learned it from colonizer perspectives. Learn history from Indigenous perspectives. Ask teachers to consider teaching about Indigenous cultures.

> Create a club. Encourage Indigenous people to join. Learn more about Indigenous rights issues. Read books by Indigenous people.

Most places are named after White men.
Activists want to change this.

CHAPTER 2

RECLAIM INDIGENOUS NAMES

Colonizers came. They named places. In doing so, they often replaced Indigenous names. They erased Indigenous people's connection to the land. Indigenous rights activists want to **reclaim** these names. Reclaim means to get something back.

Len Necefer is Navajo. He goes on outdoor adventures. He takes pictures. He shares the pictures on social media. He uses the Indigenous place names. He's creating tags.

The tallest mountain in North America is Denali. Denali means "The Great One." It is a part of creation stories of the Native Alaskan Koyukon people. In 1917, the United States renamed it Mount McKinley. In 1975, Alaskan lawmakers pushed to change its name back. In 2015, they won. Mount McKinley was changed back to Denali.

GET INSPIRED

BY LEGAL VICTORIES

○ In the 1860s, the U.S. government removed many Native American children from their families. They forced the children to go to boarding schools. These schools taught them to be more "White." Children couldn't use their languages and names. Native Americans saw these schools as the total removal of their culture. They resisted. They refused to enroll their children. In 1978, the Indian Child Welfare Act passed. Native American parents gained legal right to refuse this type of education.

○ The Ogiek people live in Kenya. They live in the Mau Forest. They're one of the last forest-dwelling communities. They rely on the forests for their food, home, and identity. They've been slowly kicked off their lands. They sued the government. They fought in court for 8 years. In 2017, the African Court of Human and Peoples Rights ruled for the Ogiek people. This is the first time the African court ruled on an Indigenous peoples' rights case.

Colonizers had a hard time pronouncing Indigenous names. They changed the names. Indigenous activists are changing their names back. Ka'nhehsí:io Deer is a Canadian journalist. She was called Jessica. She reclaimed her Mohawk name. She said, "It is a daily reminder that I am a part of a living culture."

Indigenous names and images are misused. Activists want sports teams to change their names. They want sports teams and schools to change their **mascots**. Mascots are team symbols. Having Indigenous names and images as

Feathers are important to Native Americans. They should not be used in logos.

mascots is harmful. Mascots often represent **stereotypes** about Native people. Stereotypes are ideas about a group of people based on unfair judgments. Philip Yenyo protested the use of the Chief Wahoo mascot by the Cleveland Indians. He said, "I would like to see the name and logo changed. Both have to go." He talked to fans. He sent demands to team owners. Chief Wahoo was last used in 2018. The team name will be dropped after the 2021 season.

Activists boycott companies that sponsor racist sports teams.

Stand Up, Speak Out

The Washington Redskins is a football team. "Redskins" is a racist word for Native Americans. For years, activists have fought against the name. They protested. In 2020, the team finally changed their name. Activists want people to respect their cultures. You can help!

› Check out local schools and teams. See if any of them have Indigenous names, mascots, or logos. If so, send letters or emails to the teams. Ask them to change their names.

› **Boycott** teams and companies that use Indigenous names, mascots, or logos. Boycott means to avoid or not buy something as a protest. Don't spend your money to support them. Tell others to do the same.

› Host community meetings. Tell people about the harm of using Indigenous names, mascots, or logos.

The border wall prevents travel. This travel is traditional for some religious ceremonies.

CHAPTER 3

SUPPORT FREEDOM TO MOVE

Some cultures are **nomadic**. Nomads are groups of people. They don't live in one place. They travel from place to place. They use the land to survive.

Colonizers limit freedom of movement. They create borders. They create laws that enforce borders. They allow people to own lands. Nomadic people can't move as freely. This means they have less food. They also have to change their lifestyles.

The Tohono O'odham Nation stretches from Arizona to Mexico. Its members travel through both countries. The U.S. government has started building a border wall. This divides families. It destroys cultures. Activists are speaking out. They're protesting.

Mongolia is in Asia. Mongolians are nomadic.

GET IN THE KNOW

KNOW THE HISTORY

○ **1938** The Day of Mourning took place in Australia on January 26. It was the first major protest by Australia's Indigenous people. It was hosted by Aboriginal activist groups. Activists protested the colonization by the British. They mourned the loss of their freedoms. They marched in silent protest. They wore black.

○ **1969** For 19 months, about 89 Native American activists took over Alcatraz Island near San Francisco, California. They lived on the island. They called themselves Indians of All Tribes. They reclaimed the land. They wanted to turn it into a community center. Many believe this was the start of the modern Native American rights movement.

○ **2007** The United Nations adopted the Declaration on the Rights of Indigenous Peoples. More than 140 countries signed it. This Declaration set standards for the treatment of Indigenous people. It includes the right to protect culture. It includes land rights and the right to health care.

● The Kazakh live in the mountains of western Mongolia. They use eagles to hunt.

They live in the grasslands. They're herders who move around as they follow their **livestock**. Livestock are farm animals. Khanbogd is a region in the Gobi Desert in southern Mongolia. Gold and copper were found in the region in 2001. A mining company took the land. This limited the Mongolians' freedom to move.

In 2013, Indigenous Mongolian herders fought back. They protested in front of the mines. They shouted, "Stop mining." They took the mining company owners to court. They joined with an activist group called Gobi Soil. They fought in court for 4 years. In 2017, they signed an agreement. This agreement will help protect the land. The herders want to protect their cultures for their children.

● Language and traditions are important to Indigenous people.

Stand Up, Speak Out

Some Indigenous cultures are losing their languages. They're forced to speak their colonizer's language. EllaMae Looney works with Native youth in Oregon. She is a member of the Yakama Nation. She is learning 3 Indigenous languages. She inspires others. Activists want to save languages and cultures. You can help!

> Host language classes. Host culture classes. Invite Indigenous people to lead them.

> Form a language club. Practice listening. Practice speaking. Watch movies in that language if you can. Surround yourself with the language.

> Host opportunities to use the language. Support Indigenous art. Write poetry and stories. Sing songs. Host open mic events.

The Grand Canyon was called *Ongtupqa* in the Hopi language. It's a sacred site. It's seen as a passageway to the afterlife.

CHAPTER 4

SAVE SACRED LANDS

Indigenous people have strong links to their lands and resources. Some of their land is **sacred**. Sacred means holy or special. Colonizers ignore this. This is disrespectful.

Nemonte Nenquimo is from Ecuador. She leads the Waorani Nation. Oil drilling companies wanted her land. Nenquimo said, "Our land is our home. It's sacred and it has given us life for thousands of years." She united various Indigenous groups. She asked people around the world to sign a petition. She sued the government. In court, she wore traditional clothes. She painted her face red. She brought a spear. She sang traditional songs. In 2019, she won. She protected 500,000 acres (202,343 hectares) of Amazon rainforest.

GET INVOLVED

Several groups work to protect Indigenous rights. Connect with them to get more involved.

- **Cultural Survival** fights for Indigenous rights. They partner with communities. They work to keep cultures alive. They provide resources and support.

- **Honor the Earth** creates awareness and support for Indigenous environmental issues. Its members fight for cultural survival. They promote music, arts, and media.

- **Native Hope** addresses the injustice done to Native Americans. The group promotes storytelling. It also promotes programs that heal and inspire hope.

- **The NYLA** is Native Youth Leadership Alliance. Its members provide culturally based training. They provide resources. They want to help youth become community leaders.

- **One Mind Youth Movement** is a group of youth leaders. They helped start the Standing Rock protests. They educate youth about the power of their voice.

BE kind to every kind

The Dakota Access Pipeline is a 1,172-mile (1,886 kilometer) underground tunnel. It transports oil. It stretches across North Dakota, South Dakota, Iowa, and Illinois. It runs near the Standing Rock Sioux community. It cuts through sacred lands. It could pollute the water sources. Starting in 2016, activists went to Standing Rock. They set up camps. They protested. They used their bodies to stop

● Mauna Kea is the tallest mountain in Hawaii. It's a sacred site. Activists are protesting against the building of a telescope there.

drilling. They were attacked. They sued. Jasilyn Charger is part of the Cheyenne River Sioux tribe. She started an activist youth group. She hosted a run from North Dakota to Washington, D.C. She delivered a petition. She raised awareness.

Map your land. Learn about the hunting trails. Learn about the medicinal plants.

Stand Up, Speak Out

Acknowledge means to accept. Land acknowledgments are formal statements. They're ways to honor Indigenous lands and people. Indigenous people practice acknowledging the land. Activists want us to do this as well. You can help!

> Identify the native lands on which you live. Learn about the Indigenous people.

> Write a land acknowledgment: "This event is taking place on traditional ___ land. This land belongs to the ___ people. These people have protected the land for generations."

> State the land acknowledgment. Do this before all events or meetings. This will raise awareness about histories and cultures that have been silenced.

GLOSSARY

acknowledge (ak-NOL-ij) to accept or to admit as truth

activists (AK-tih-vists) people who fight for political or social change

boycott (BOI-kot) to refuse to buy something or take part in

causes (KAWZ-es) the reasons for activism

colonization (kah-luh-nuh-ZAY-shuhn) the forceful takeover by another country or group of settlers

genocide (JEH-nuh-syde) the killing of many people from a specific group

Indigenous (in-DIH-juh-nuhss) originating in a particular place, native

justice (JUHSS-tiss) the upholding of what is fair and right

livestock (LIVE-stok) farm animals

mascots (MASS-kots) people or things that are supposed to bring good luck or that are used to symbolize an event or team

nomadic (NOH-mad-ick) moving from place to place

reclaim (rih-KLAYM) to get something back

reservation (rez-ur-VAY-shuhn) an area of land set aside by the U.S. government

sacred (SAY-krid) holy and deserving of respect

stereotypes (STERR-ee-oh-TYPS) ideas about a group of people based on unfair judgments

strikes (STRYKES) organized protests where people refuse to do something

LEARN MORE!

Dunbar-Ortiz, Roxanne. *An Indigenous Peoples' History of the United States: For Young People.* Boston, MA: Beacon Press, 2019.

O'Brien, Cynthia. *National Geographic Kids Encyclopedia of American Indian History and Culture: Stories, Timelines, Maps, and More.* Washington, D.C.: National Geographic Kids, 2019.

Sorell, Traci, and Frane Lessac (illust.). *We Are Still Here!: Native American Truths Everyone Should Know.* Watertown, MA: Charlesbridge, 2021.

INDEX